CONFORMED

INTO THE LIKENESS OF CHRIST

30 Day Devotional

Nate Stevens

Copyright © 2021 by Nate Stevens

All rights reserved. No part of this publication may be reproduced, distributed, or transmitted in any form or by any means, including photocopying, recording, or other electronic or mechanical methods, without the prior written permission of the publisher, except in the case of brief quotations embodied in critical reviews and certain other noncommercial uses permitted by copyright law. For permission requests, write to the publisher at publishing@kingdomwinds.com.

Unless otherwise indicated, Scripture quotations are from The New King James Version (NKJV) / Thomas Nelson Publishers, Nashville: Thomas Nelson Publishers. Copyright © 1982. Used by permission. All rights reserved.

Scripture quotations marked (NLT) are taken from the Holy Bible, New Living Translation, copyright © 1996, 2004, 2015 by Tyndale House Foundation. Used by permission of Tyndale House Publishers, a Division of Tyndale House Ministries, Carol Stream, Illinois 60188. All rights reserved.

First Edition, 2021
ISBN 10:
ISBN 13:

Published by Kingdom Winds Publishing.
6 Charleston Oak Lane, Greenville, SC 29615
www.kingdomwinds.com
publishing@kingdomwinds.com
Printed in the United States of America.

Cover Design by Christine Dupre

The views expressed in this book are not necessarily those of the publisher.

ACKNOWLEDGEMENT

First and foremost, thank you, Jesus Christ, my Lord and Savior, for graciously conforming me from what I was and gradually into what You envision me becoming. Not only do You love me as You found me, You also love me enough to shape, mold, and conform me into Your likeness! What an amazing work of grace!

Additionally, thank you, Karen Stevens, for seemingly endless hours watching me study, research, and write, then helping choose which devotions to include as well as develop the cover concept. Along with my heart, you have my thanks and appreciation. I love you!

Finally, thank you, Gary and Elizabeth Suess and the Kingdom Winds family for your partnership in this endeavor. I am grateful for your vision and ministry to support authors, songwriters, artists, and others as they fulfill their roles in building and equipping the eternal Kingdom of God. Bless you!

ENDORSEMENTS

I love Conformed: Into the Likeness of Christ, especially the space for daily notes and journaling. Beautifully thought out and amazing to read, every day is uplifting and leads us to pursue the likeness of Christ. Everyday examples with direct support from Scripture encourage a closer walk with God.

Phyllis Runyon, Singles Coordinator
Celebration Church—Blountville, TN

Every true believer desires to think, talk, act, and be more like our Savior Jesus Christ. In his devotional, Conformed: Into the Likeness of Christ, Nate Stevens leads the reader on a 30-day path to achieve that goal in our ultimate pursuit of being more like Jesus.

Wendy Griffith, 700 Club Co-host
Author of "You Are a Prize to be Won, Don't Settle for Less than God's Best"

INTRODUCTION

Conforming is a battle! My will, unless crucified, is in constant conflict with God's will.

God created, called, and purposes us to be conformed into His likeness. "He chose us in Him before the foundation of the world, that we should be holy and without blame before Him in love" (Ephesians 1:4). "Whom He foreknew, He also predestined *to be* conformed to the image of His Son" (Romans 8:29).

The word "transformed" in the Bible is a Greek word (metamorphoo) that implies a divine, supernatural metamorphosis. It generally refers to the spiritual regeneration, transfiguring, or transformation the Holy Spirit undertakes internally in the lives of believers. However, "conformed" is a different Greek word (summorphoo). It means being conformable, assimilated, fashioned, or molded to a desired shape or likeness. Both terms describe spiritual processes; however, conformity quite often involves the personal choice of external change.

Coupled with the Holy Spirit's inner transformation, every believer holds the responsibility to conform to Christlikeness. This involves daily taking up the cross, "putting off" anything not Christlike, and "putting on" of Christlike characteristics and behaviors (Ephesians 4:17-32). It is the daily dying to self and submitting, or conforming, to the new life in Christ and walking in alignment with God's Word.

Conforming to His likeness is more than an emotional experience or even an intellectual encounter with God. It is a growing, intense desire to be like Christ—His likeness, His thoughts, His Spirit, His presence permeating every area, aspect, and decision of life. Only in this way do I increasingly resemble Him, am conformed into His image, and am positioned for eternity with Him. "We also eagerly wait for the Savior, the Lord Jesus Christ, who will transform our lowly body that it may be conformed to His glorious body" (Philippians 3:20-21).

These concise daily devotions encourage such a conforming encounter. May they be daily echoes of Jesus' call to follow and imitate Him. More than just reading them daily, I encourage you to meditate on them—applying them to life and allowing them to ignite a deeper, more intimate walk with God.

Above all else, may this 30-day journey encourage you to embrace God's ongoing work of conforming you "to the image of His Son" (Romans 8:29).

Nate Stevens

CONFORMED TO CHRIST – DAY 1

Who Am I Following? (Isaiah 45:2)

God says, "I will go before you and make the crooked places straight." His promise is twofold: to lead me and to straighten my journey. Though sometimes confusing to human hearts and minds, His ways are never crooked, impassible, or suspect. His ways are perfect and straight, even when they seem perplexing or not readily visible. My challenge is to follow where He leads—embracing His transforming, conforming work in my life. If He is not leading, who am I following? If my journey seems twisted, dangerous, or dark, am I on His pathway or trails of my own choosing? Yes, His way often involves risk, adversity, surrender, and trust. However, if He is leading, I can trust His heart and follow accordingly.

Father, along with Your call to follow You, calm my anxious heart and mind with Your "Fear not."

CONFORMED TO CHRIST JOURNAL – DAY 1

How am I living in conformity to Christ in all areas of my life? In what area is He working on me?

_____

_____

_____

_____

_____

_____

_____

_____

_____

_____

CONFORMED TO CHRIST – DAY 2

Developing Christlikeness (Hebrews 11:1)

"Now faith is the substance of things hoped for, the evidence of things not seen." Love is not developed by positive personalities—it grows from loving the unlovely. Joy is not developed by cheerful circumstances—it grows from inner contentment though living with unmet expectations and hardship. Peace is not developed by mystical meditations—it grows from resolute serenity in the midst of chaos. Obedience is not developed by forced submission—it grows by rejecting opportunities to disobey. Patience is not developed by structured tolerance—it grows from calm persistence during frustrating delays. Character is not developed by planned performance—it grows by consistency in increasing adversity. Faith is not developed by preconceived belief—it grows with each determined step into the invisible.

Father, please continually develop Christlike characteristics in me.

CONFORMED TO CHRIST JOURNAL – DAY 2

Which Christlike characteristic is my strongest / weakest? How am I yielding to His likeness?

_____

_____

_____

_____

_____

_____

_____

_____

_____

CONFORMED TO CHRIST – DAY 3

*Everything I Need, Nothing I Lack
(Psalm 23:1-2)*

When God is my shepherd, He brings me to a place of satisfaction and quenching. As His sheep, He leads me beside (not to) still waters and causes me to lie down (not graze) in green pastures. Being disinterested by calm, refreshing water and lush, green pastures implies I am already full. In Him, I have all I need and lack nothing. But this is a learned, matured mindset developed by experience in following Him. Young and immature sheep generally get distracted by thirst or hunger. The distractions of worldly wants and entertainment provide meager meals. However, mature, seasoned sheep have learned to feast deeply on God's everlasting water and provision. The more I have of Him, I find He is all I need.

Heavenly Father, continue molding and maturing me to where I find abundance, contentment, and fulfillment in You alone.

CONFORMED TO CHRIST JOURNAL – DAY 3

What worldly wants, habits, or mindsets distract or restrict my conformity to Christ?

_____

_____

_____

_____

_____

_____

_____

_____

_____

CONFORMED TO CHRIST – DAY 4

Expecting Heaven While Living Like Hell
(Ephesians 5:25-27)

When I dance on the precipice of sin, sooner or later, I lose my balance and fall. The irresistible gravitational pull eventually exceeds my resistance. As countercultural as it may seem, Christ wants a glorious church—His future Bride—to have no spot, wrinkle, or any sin stain. His Bride is to be holy and without blemish. Imagine a pure white wedding gown with no stains whatsoever—no coffee spills, ketchup smudges, greasy French-fry hand smears, wrinkles, patches, tears—no impurities whatsoever. With that as my goal, the conforming call of Christ bids me to resist and altogether avoid the tempting chasm of sin.

Father, as Your follower, may my life display such a pure, unblemished, holy witness that I reflect You in a dark and dying world. Help me shine Your light— not in self-centered pursuits, but through Your righteousness and sanctification.

CONFORMED TO CHRIST JOURNAL – DAY 4

What tempting call of sin beckons me to compromise my walk and witness? How am I confronting it?

_____

_____

_____

_____

_____

_____

_____

_____

_____

CONFORMED TO CHRIST – DAY 5

Maintaining Christlikeness in the World
(Ezra 2:59, 62)

When the Israelites returned from Babylonian captivity, they recorded the genealogy of each family. This exercise identified those with Hebrew heritage, as well as those who qualified for the priesthood. For whatever reason, one people group could not confirm their identity. Their ancestral records may have been lost or not deemed valuable enough to safeguard during captivity. Maybe the individuals involved blended in with their foreign surroundings and forgot who they were. No matter the reason, their lost identity hindered their purpose. God calls His followers to "Come out from among them and be separate" (2 Corinthians 6:17)—a call to Christlikeness.

Father, by separating myself from the world and shining Your light as evidence of Your spiritual heritage, I reflect Your family resemblance. May my identity mirror You today.

CONFORMED TO CHRIST JOURNAL – DAY 5

How does my conformity and identity with Christ help to overcome the world and shine His light?

_____

_____

_____

_____

_____

_____

_____

_____

_____

_____

CONFORMED TO CHRIST – DAY 6

*Recognizing the Voice of Jesus
(John 10:27)*

Jesus said, "My sheep hear My voice...and they follow Me." If it were not socially acceptable to attend church, if family or friends did not believe in God, if all I had was my Bible, would I love and follow Him? Being a Christian is not a family hand-me-down relationship, societal expectation, status symbol, or even a mental disposition based on paintings and murals of Jesus. A genuine Christ-follower recognizes the Shepherd's voice, surrenders entirely to Him, and immediately follows Him. Recognizing someone's voice involves distinguishing it from all other voices. Authentic believers hear and follow Jesus through obedience to His Word. If Jesus walked by today and called my name, would I recognize His voice? To conform to His likeness, I must first hear.

*Holy Father, tune my heart and mind to Your voice.
May I instantly hear and follow You.*

CONFORMED TO CHRIST JOURNAL – DAY 6

How is God speaking with me today? How am I responding to conform to His will and likeness?

_____

_____

_____

_____

_____

_____

_____

_____

_____

CONFORMED TO CHRIST – DAY 7

*Sometimes God Grants My Foolish Desires
(1 Samuel 8)*

Even after logical appeals and spiritual warnings, the Israelites demanded a king. They wanted to be like the surrounding nations. No longer valuing or wanting God's theocracy, they sought a physical king they could visibly see and access. Ignoring Samuel's solemn counsel and warning, they laser-focused on their desire. So, God gave in, fully knowing the consequences of their choice. He acknowledged their rebellion: "They have rejected Me, that I should not reign over them" (1 Samuel 8:7). Oh, how often my desires lead me away from my loving Father and His best for me. Yet conforming to His likeness involves my continual submission to His will.

Dear God, help me reject any choice You have not sanctioned, any decision You have not approved, any thought not captive to Your mind, and any action that would break Your heart.

CONFORMED TO CHRIST JOURNAL – DAY 7

How am I yielding my preferences, decisions, choices, thoughts, and actions to God's perfect will?

_____

_____

_____

_____

_____

_____

_____

_____

_____

CONFORMED TO CHRIST – DAY 8

What Dominates My Heart? (Matthew 6:21)

"Where your treasure is, there your heart will be also." What I value most is what dominates my heart. When my heart is full of Jesus, He will bleed into all aspects of my life. Equally, when I fill my heart with fear, pride, bitterness, self-interests, doubt, gossip, regret, lies, or anything else, those will also flow through all my life connections. Jesus said what dominates a person's speech exposes the condition of that person's heart. "What you say flows from what is in your heart" (Luke 6:45, NLT). What I persistently talk about, the lifestyle I consistently live, and the priorities I pursue reveal what I value most in my heart.

Oh, God, please dominate my heart. May You overshadow every interaction, season every conversation, and establish every priority. Fill my mouth, heart, and life with You and only You.

CONFORMED TO CHRIST JOURNAL – DAY 8

What dominates my thoughts and conversations today? What does it reveal about my heart?

_____

_____

_____

_____

_____

_____

_____

_____

_____

CONFORMED TO CHRIST – DAY 9

Living Blamelessly Before God (Genesis 17:1)

"I am Almighty God; walk before Me and be blameless." When Abraham was ninety-nine years old, God reiterated His covenant to bless him and make him the father of many nations. With this covenant came the condition of walking blamelessly before God. Far from being a requirement of sinless perfection, this stipulation involved living with moral integrity and truth—maintaining an upright, full, and sincere lifestyle before God. A supernaturally transformed and conformed life! Paul helped explain: "Walk worthy of the Lord, fully pleasing *Him*, being fruitful in every good work and increasing in the knowledge of God" (Colossians 1:10). It is a lifestyle of humble godliness, gratitude, and grace as I let God's Holy Spirit, Life, and Light shine through me.

Father God, help me live blamelessly before You.

CONFORMED TO CHRIST JOURNAL – DAY 9

How is God shining through me today? How am I pleasing Him in all my interactions?

_____

_____

_____

_____

_____

_____

_____

_____

_____

CONFORMED TO CHRIST – DAY 10

Standing in Liberty—Walking in the Spirit
(Galatians 5:16)

"Walk in the Spirit, and you shall not fulfill the lust of the flesh." While standing in the liberty Christ gives (Galatians 5:1), Christians also walk in the power of the Spirit. Standing is a resolute position; walking is a determined pursuit. Genuine believers stand unyielding in their position in Christ, then walk passionately under the guidance of the Holy Spirit. God's Word gives spiritual enlightenment (Psalm 119:105) and the Spirit guides into all truth (John 16:13). With hearts and minds receptive and yielded to God's Word and Spirit, lifestyles exhibit spiritual fruit: "Love, joy, peace, longsuffering, kindness, goodness, faithfulness, gentleness, self-control" (Galatians 5:22-23).

Father God, help me walk daily with the intentional choice of allowing Your work of complete conformity of Your likeness in me.

CONFORMED TO CHRIST JOURNAL – DAY 10

How am I intentionally allowing—even actively embracing—God's transforming work in my life?

_____

_____

_____

_____

_____

_____

_____

_____

_____

_____

CONFORMED TO CHRIST – DAY 11

The Combination of Love and Holiness (Exodus 15:1-3)

"The LORD *is* my strength and song, and He has become my salvation; He is my God, and I will praise Him." God is love (1 John 4:8), yet He is also holy (1 Peter 1:16). Too often, I can grow complacent with the concept of a loving God while overlooking His uncompromising holiness. It is easy to confuse His love with tolerance for sinful desires, preferences, and lifestyles. As loving as He is, God is also a "man of war" (Exodus 15:3). He protects His own while opposing those who flaunt their wickedness and parade their evil desires. He is "not willing that any should perish" (2 Peter 3:9), but He also restricts His mercy when the time for judgment arrives.

Father, in Your great love, help me become more holy, more like Jesus, each and every day.

CONFORMED TO CHRIST JOURNAL – DAY 11

How are God's love and holiness co-existing in my life? How am I demonstrating both today?

_____

_____

_____

_____

_____

_____

_____

_____

_____

CONFORMED TO CHRIST – DAY 12

*The Joy and Challenge of Living by Faith
(Galatians 3:11)*

"The just shall live by faith." Christians are called to a walk of faith—for salvation, guidance, provision, and eternity. It is not a walk of works to earn God's righteousness; nor is it a walk by sight where everything is clearly seen. Living by faith involves implicitly trusting God. It is joyous to experience the blessings the Heavenly Father offers. But my walk with God is also challenging as I wrestle with uncertainty and lack of control. My faith grows proportionally as I trust God for what I cannot see or do on my own. To stretch and strengthen me, He orchestrates events and circumstances that provide growth opportunities for my faith. His ultimate goal remains the same—shaping me into His likeness.

Father, I love and trust You and welcome Your conforming opportunities.

CONFORMED TO CHRIST JOURNAL – DAY 12

How does my faith in God grow when I yield control of my life to Him? What am I giving Him today?

_____

_____

_____

_____

_____

_____

_____

_____

_____

CONFORMED TO CHRIST – DAY 13

The Reflection of God's Presence
(Exodus 34:29)

"The skin of his face shone while he talked with Him." While spending time with God, during the second writing of the Ten Commandments, Moses physically absorbed God's presence and energy. When he returned to the Israelites, his skin glowed and they were afraid to get near him. To accommodate them, Moses covered his face with a veil. Such is the power and magnificence of spending quality time with God Almighty. Being infused with God's presence and Spirit may not make my face shine like the sun, but my life will radiate His glory as a witness of my intimacy with Him. Shine through me, oh Heavenly Father!

Father God, please help me shine Your light before men, that they may see my good works and holy lifestyle and then glorify You (Matthew 5:16).

CONFORMED TO CHRIST JOURNAL – DAY 13

How am I reflecting God's presence and likeness in my life today? How is His light shining through me?

_____

_____

_____

_____

_____

_____

_____

_____

_____

_____

CONFORMED TO CHRIST – DAY 14

Walking Without Reservation or Hesitation
(Colossians 1:10)

"Walk worthy of the Lord, fully pleasing *Him*, being fruitful in every good work and increasing in the knowledge of God." The call to a walk of holiness encompasses every aspect of life. It includes a person's vocation and calling (Ephesians 4:1) as well as conduct and lifestyle (Philippians 1:27). Ultimately, Christians are to walk worthy of God (1 Thessalonians 2:12). This supersedes all personal preferences, cultural trends, even denominational nuances that do not align with His Word. By placing God as my primary audience, I seek to please Him alone and turn my back on the expectations and applause of man. I do so, not from fear or obligation, but from a grateful heart fully surrendered to Him—which is my reasonable service (Romans 12:1).

Father, may I faithfully, boldly, and unashamedly walk worthy of You.

CONFORMED TO CHRIST JOURNAL – DAY 14

In which areas of life am I hesitant to fully surrender to God? How can I change to walk worthy of Him?

_____

_____

_____

_____

_____

_____

_____

_____

_____

CONFORMED TO CHRIST – DAY 15

Wrestling Toward Conformity
(Genesis 32:24)

"Then Jacob was left alone; and a Man wrestled with him until the breaking of day." In an attempt to appease his estranged brother, Esau, Jacob strategically divided his family and possessions into separate groups. He sent each group ahead of him until he was left alone. That was when God met him. After struggling all night, Jacob refused to release God until God blessed him. When asked for his name, Jacob could have withheld his identity; however, he honestly admitted—supplanter. But God transformed him, granting a new name and identity. No longer a supplanter or deceiver, he would now be Israel—prince with God. God does not merely change me; thankfully, He transforms me completely.

God, may I never stop pursuing You until You transform me with Your holy identity. Please continue Your work until Christ is formed in me.

CONFORMED TO CHRIST JOURNAL – DAY 15

How passionate is my pursuit of Christlikeness? Am I embracing or quenching the Spirit's transformation?

_____

_____

_____

_____

_____

_____

_____

_____

_____

CONFORMED TO CHRIST – DAY 16

Always Pursuing What is Good
(1 Thessalonians 5:15)

"Always pursue what is good both for yourselves and for all." A pursuit involves intentionality, a specific goal, and the unyielding determination to achieve it. Paul encourages Christians to have such a strategic pursuit of what is good. This "good" implies what is beneficial as opposed to what is harmful or bad. It incorporates the Golden Rule as well as the defining characteristic of a Christian—love (John 13:35). Jesus said His followers love their enemies, bless those who curse them, do good to those who hate them, and pray for those who falsely accuse and persecute them (Matthew 5:44). He set the standard by always "doing good" (Acts 10:38). Living in holiness is not always easy, but it is always good.

Heavenly Father, empower me to model the heart, hands, and feet of Jesus to a hurting and lost world.

CONFORMED TO CHRIST JOURNAL - DAY 16

Why is it difficult to model holiness at all times? How does the Holy Spirit help in this effort?

_____

_____

_____

_____

_____

_____

_____

_____

_____

CONFORMED TO CHRIST – DAY 17

Aligning My Plans with God's Plans
(Genesis 15:4)

"This one shall not be your heir, but one who will come from your own body shall be your heir." Abraham was a wise, successful, wealthy man. As such, he properly arranged the details of his estate. Being childless, he identified Eliezer of Damascus as his heir. However, God had other plans. Abraham made his decision based on human logic and conventional wisdom. Yet, God sovereignly orchestrated him to become the father of the Israelites with innumerable descendants through his promised son, Isaac. It is wise to make prudent plans and strategic decisions; however, involving God in them all is the best option. "In all your ways acknowledge Him, and He shall direct your paths" (Proverbs 3:6).

Father, please align my thoughts, plans, and strategies with Your ultimate purpose.

CONFORMED TO CHRIST JOURNAL – DAY 17

What plans of mine are in God's hands? How does trusting Him increase my faith and likeness to Him?

_____

_____

_____

_____

_____

_____

_____

_____

_____

CONFORMED TO CHRIST – DAY 18

Holy, Blameless, and Loving (Ephesians 1:4b)

"Be holy and without blame before Him in love." What a difference it would make if all Christians demonstrated authentic lifestyles that were loving, sacred, morally pure, and without a hint of blame. As I live each moment in God's presence, His righteousness and love should become my distinguishing characteristics (John 13:35). As a Christian, I should live a holy, blameless, and loving lifestyle because I bear His family resemblance. He created me for intimate fellowship with Him. Such intimacy only exists in the absence of habitual sin (His righteousness), pure lifestyles (conformity to Him), and a pursuit of His presence (intimacy). God makes me holy because He is holy (1 Peter 1:15-16). He is preparing me as part of His pure, unblemished bride for eternity (Ephesians 5:27).

Holy Father, please continue molding me with Your holiness, righteousness, and love.

CONFORMED TO CHRIST JOURNAL – DAY 18

What am I doing today to walk in God's holiness, righteousness, and love? How is He molding me?

_____

_____

_____

_____

_____

_____

_____

_____

_____

CONFORMED TO CHRIST – DAY 19

Judging Others Inflicts Harm on All Involved
(Psalm 66:18)

"If I regard iniquity in my heart, The Lord will not hear." Self-righteous judgment hurts both the receiver and giver. It is impossible to clasp hands in prayer while throwing stones at others. It is impossible to genuinely worship God while harboring vengeful and bitter thoughts toward others. It is impossible to fully love others while holding on to past hurt, betrayal, or unjust attack. It is impossible to live an abundant, transformed life while destroying the lives of others. As Jesus cautioned, it is far better to resolve the plank in my eye before worrying about the speck of sawdust in someone else's eye.

Father, help me be harsh with myself and lovingly truthful and kind with others. When necessity demands it, help me judge righteously (John 7:24).

CONFORMED TO CHRIST JOURNAL - DAY 19

What judgments, grudges, or past hurts am I harboring? How is God prompting me to forgive?

_____

_____

_____

_____

_____

_____

_____

_____

_____

CONFORMED TO CHRIST – DAY 20

Imitating God (Ephesians 5:1)

"Be imitators of God as dear children." It is challenging, nearly impossible, to imitate someone I do not know personally and intimately. To imitate God is to reflect His image as in a mirror—His character, mannerism, thoughts, tone, poise, and likeness. To do so, I must be born of God, know Him experientially (not just about Him), and surrender to His leading. Imitating or exhibiting God involves holiness and "walking in love" fully and unconditionally as He loves me. As the moon reflects the sun's light, God's light shines through me. His Holy Spirit resides in me. As His child, I bear the Family resemblance. My goal is to imitate my Heavenly Father in all aspects of life.

Loving Father, in my passionate pursuit of You, help me reject all sinful influences in my life. Purify me so I may reflect You in all my interactions.

CONFORMED TO CHRIST JOURNAL – DAY 20

What am I doing to deepen my intimacy and fellowship with God? How am I imitating Him?

_____

_____

_____

_____

_____

_____

_____

_____

_____

_____

CONFORMED TO CHRIST – DAY 21

Softening Hardened Hearts (Genesis 42:21)

"We saw the anguish of his soul when he pleaded with us, and we would not hear." When Joseph's brothers went to buy food in Egypt, Joseph recognized them. As a test, he treated them harshly and accused them of being spies. Immediately, pricked by guilt, they knew exactly why he was treating them this way. They recalled their callous, hardhearted response to young Joseph's cries for mercy. Oh, to have a heart filled with compassion for the hurting and mercy for the oppressed. "I will take the heart of stone out...and give you a heart of flesh" (Ezekiel 36:26). Change my heart, oh God!

Loving Father, may I extend mercy and compassion when in my power to do so (Proverbs 3:27), gratefully realizing You extend these so graciously to me. Grant me a heart modeled after Your own.

CONFORMED TO CHRIST JOURNAL – DAY 21

How is God softening my heart? In what ways do I extend the love, mercy, and grace God gives me?

CONFORMED TO CHRIST – DAY 22

No Sense of Entitlement (Galatians 2:20)

There is no place in the life of a follower of Jesus for personal rights, a sense of superiority, or condemning legalism. While living the Christian life here on earth, I am a citizen and ambassador of Heaven (Philippians 3:20). Here, I am no better than anyone else, simply forgiven and clothed in righteousness—neither of which I deserve. My anticipated heavenly inheritance only empowers and energizes my earthly service. God does not love me more than unbelievers. He seeks to save to the uttermost, even the most wicked. I hold no claim other than acceptance and appropriation of what Christ did on the Cross on my behalf. From this place of gratitude and humility, He calls me to willingly follow Him and lovingly serve others, all while yielding to His work in me.

Loving Father, may my distinguishing characteristic always be love for You and others, never superiority, personal rights, or entitlement.

CONFORMED TO CHRIST JOURNAL – DAY 22

What spiritual entitlement or superior mindset prevents me from conforming fully to Christlikeness?

_____

_____

_____

_____

_____

_____

_____

_____

_____

CONFORMED TO CHRIST – DAY 23

The Path to Humility (Exodus 10:3)

"How long will you refuse to humble yourself before Me?" God posed this question to Pharaoh in response to his arrogant refusal to free the Israelites. As God's judgments intensified, I am amazed at Pharaoh's stubbornness. Yet, I often struggle with my own resistance when God calls me to a closer walk of holiness. I've come to realize that any refusal of the divine is usually centered around pride. I often overlook that God resists the proud but gives grace to the humble (James 4:6). When full of myself, God humbles me; when I humble myself before Him, He lifts me up in due time (1 Peter 5:6). God honors me only when I forsake stubborn pride and begin the path to sincere humility.

Father, I humbly thank you for Your goodness and discipline and seek to humbly follow, surrender, serve, and imitate You.

CONFORMED TO CHRIST JOURNAL - DAY 23

How might the subtle sin of pride be creeping into my life? How do I confront and overcome it?

CONFORMED TO CHRIST – DAY 24

*The Closer to Jesus, the Thinner the Crowd
(John 6)*

At the beginning of John 6, Jesus feeds more than five thousand people. They followed Him—yes, probably to hear Him speak, but I suspect most followed for the benefits He provided. Free food, free healing, free spiritual teaching—why not follow? However, by the end of the chapter, the crowds are gone, family members have deserted Him; only the disciples remain. The longer I follow Jesus, the closer I get to Him, the more I align my life to His moral standard and purpose, the reality is that fewer people will walk with me. The journey of God's holiness may separate friends and family. They may not hear or heed His call to deeper intimacy. Yet, as Jesus counseled Peter (John 21:22), I must not worry about others. I must just get closer to Jesus.

Father, draw me ever closer to You each day. I hear Your call and long for Your intimacy.

CONFORMED TO CHRIST JOURNAL – DAY 24

How does my faithful, deliberate pursuit of intimacy with God supernaturally separate me from others?

_____

_____

_____

_____

_____

_____

_____

_____

CONFORMED TO CHRIST – DAY 25

Keep Walking (Deuteronomy 11:24)

"Every place on which the sole of your foot treads shall be yours." In God's promise to give the Israelites the Promised Land as their possession, He inserted a sub-promise to give them whatever land upon which they walked. To expand their boundaries, He would reward their courage and faith in Him. The Christian walk holds similar promise. God promises never to forsake me and has given the Holy Spirit to indwell, comfort, guide, and instruct me. He commands me to share His Gospel of peace with all nations. God encourages me to press toward the prize of His high calling. He urges me to walk in the newness of His life. Ultimately, He continues transforming me until I conform to the likeness of Jesus (Romans 8:29). My goal is to keep on walking in and with Him every moment.

Father, help me walk faithfully and intentionally in ongoing conformity with Your likeness.

CONFORMED TO CHRIST JOURNAL – DAY 25

How closely aligned are my daily walk and lifestyle with God's transforming process of Christlikeness?

CONFORMED TO CHRIST – DAY 26

The Father's Watchful Care (Philippians 2:22)

"As a son with his father he served with me in the gospel." In commending Timothy for his faithful service, the Apostle Paul reveals the participation Christians have with God in His work. Whatever a father does, his child watches. At the appropriate time, the child tries to imitate what the father is doing. Working beside him, the father guides and instructs to hone the child's skills and knowledge. In like fashion, I serve my Heavenly Father. From His Word and work, I observe His character and quality of work, becoming acquainted with Him intimately. When engaging in ministry, I work along beside Him, not resisting, complaining, or debating, but following where He leads, responding willingly to His loving wisdom and instruction.

Father, thank You for Your patience, encouragement, and instruction as I imitate You. May all I say, think, and do honor You.

CONFORMED TO CHRIST JOURNAL – DAY 26

How do I imitate my Heavenly Father? What evidence do I have of the Family's resemblance?

_____

_____

_____

_____

_____

_____

_____

_____

_____

CONFORMED TO CHRIST – DAY 27

Chosen, But Not Pampered
(Deuteronomy 6:11-15)

"When you have eaten and are full—*then* beware, lest you forget the LORD." Even though God chose the Israelites as His people, He did not grant them spiritual leniency. He often disciplined them for habitual cycles of rebellion and unfaithfulness. There was no grandfatherly winking at their wickedness. Instead, He warned, "You shall fear the LORD your God and serve Him. You shall not go after other gods...lest the anger of the LORD your God...destroy you from the face of the earth." Christians are God's "chosen generation...His own special people" (1 Peter 2:9). However, this does not grant the license to live as I please. Instead, it is a life of conformity to Christlikeness.

Father, thank you for choosing me. Instruct me in Your righteousness, discipline me in love, mold me into Your likeness, and draw me into Your presence.

CONFORMED TO CHRIST JOURNAL - DAY 27

What perceived "need" is God not meeting that keeps me reliant on Him? What is my reaction to this?

_____

_____

_____

_____

_____

_____

_____

_____

CONFORMED TO CHRIST – DAY 28

*Finding Satisfaction in God's Abundance
(Ephesians 3:19)*

"That you may be filled with all the fullness of God." Being filled is to be crammed full, complete, satisfied, or fulfilled. But being filled with God involves first an emptying, a relinquishing of all previous contents. The fullness of God is His completion, abundance, and plenty—not the accumulation of material things, but His nature and character. By emptying myself of everything but God, then allowing Him to fill me with Himself, I find the true essence of satisfaction. I become like Him, know Him fully, and have His righteous nature abundantly overflowing in my heart and life. "In Your presence *is* fullness of joy; at Your right hand *are* pleasures forevermore." (Psalm 16:11).

*I submit my dreams and desires to You, oh, Father.
Fill me with Your eternal abundance.*

CONFORMED TO CHRIST JOURNAL – DAY 28

How is God rewarding my surrender in unexpected ways? What remains to be yielded to Him?

_____

_____

_____

_____

_____

_____

_____

_____

_____

CONFORMED TO CHRIST - DAY 29

*Maintaining a Sense of Godly Reverence
(Leviticus 10:1-3)*

"This is what the LORD spoke, saying: 'By those who come near Me I must be regarded as holy.'" When Aaron's sons, Nadab and Abihu, offered "profane fire before the LORD," God's wrath erupted, killing them instantly. Their casual, presumptuous, possibly even cavalier approach to God and serving Him produced indifferent attention to detail. This casual apathy resulted in disobedience against God's clear instructions and prompted God's swift judgment. Though called and anointed, they lost their reverence for God's holiness. God may be loving, gracious, and merciful; however, He is also just, holy, and deserving of honor and reverence (Malachi 1:6). Gratitude, humility, and Godly fear promote such awe-inspiring reverence.

Father God, I approach You in humble reverence. May I never lose sight of Your awesome majesty.

CONFORMED TO CHRIST JOURNAL – DAY 29

How do I demonstrate my reverence toward God? What keeps me from presuming upon His grace?

_____

_____

_____

_____

_____

_____

_____

_____

_____

CONFORMED TO CHRIST – DAY 30

God Will Finish His Work in Me
(Genesis 28:15)

During Jacob's dream of the ladder that reached to heaven, God promised him, "I am with you and will keep you wherever you go...I will not leave you until I have done what I have spoken to you." Reassuring Jacob of the blessing passed down from Abraham and Isaac, He then repeated His covenant promise. God faithfully gives His presence and permanence when completing His work in each believer's heart and life. "Being confident of this very thing, that He who has begun a good work in you will complete it until the day of Jesus Christ" (Philippians 1:6). The secret is in allowing Him to complete the work, not resisting it. "Do not quench the Spirit" (1 Thessalonians 5:19).

Father, thank You for not abandoning me at my worst. Thank you for continually transforming me so I may stand before You robed in Your best.

CONFORMED TO CHRIST JOURNAL – DAY 30

How has this 30-day journey better conformed me to Christlikeness? What are my next steps?

_____

_____

_____

_____

_____

_____

_____

_____

_____

ABOUT THE AUTHOR

A lifelong student of Scripture, Nate Stevens has also enjoyed a banking career in various leadership roles. He is the author of *Matched 4 Life, Deck Time with Jesus*, and *Transformed: Until Christ is Formed in You* as well as a contributing author on several of the Moments Books (*Billy Graham Moments, Romantic Moments, Divine Moments, Spoken Moments, Christmas Moments, Stupid Moments,* etc.). Nate writes online articles for ChristianDevotions.us and KingdomWinds.com as well as several other ministries. Additionally, he co-founded and leads Fusion, a Christian singles ministry. A popular speaker and teacher at conferences, seminars, and Bible study groups, he speaks on a wide variety of topics. Nate has two adult children. He and his wife, Karen, live near Charlotte, North Carolina.

Follow Nate and find more resources at:
www.natestevens.net

www.ingramcontent.com/pod-product-compliance
Lightning Source LLC
Chambersburg PA
CBHW071254070526
44583CB00017B/2459